For Mom and Dad who gave me my wings;
For Bob and Mary, Brian, and Ali, who continue to help me soar!

What Color Is Your Dream?

Printed in the United States of America.

For information, please contact:
Brown Books Publishing Group
16200 North Dallas Parkway, Suite 170 • Dallas, Texas 75248
www.brownbooks.com • 972-381-0009
A New Era in Publishing™

ISBN-13: 978-1-933285-56-6
ISBN-10: 1-933285-56-7
LCCN: 2007925648
1 2 3 4 5 6 7 8 9 10

Cover Design: Ken Johnston and Kittie Beletic
Author Photograph: Mary Ann Sherman, Dallas, Texas

(for ALL, thank you, Ken!)

What Color Is your Dream?

by

Kittie Nesius Beletic

A dream begins with a wish on a star

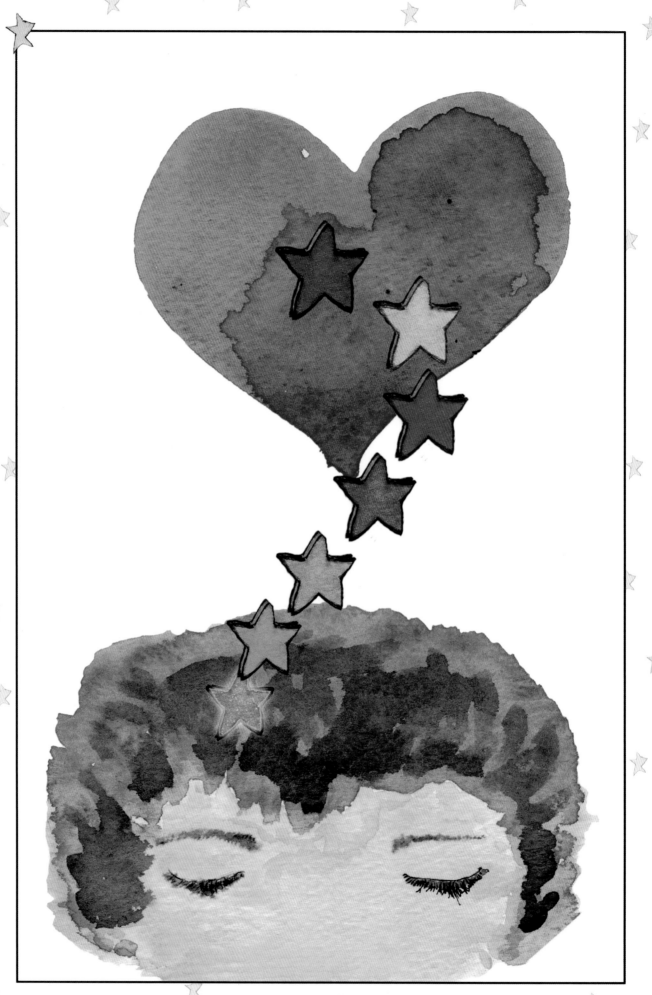

It makes its way

from your mind to your heart.

Your body will help by acting it out ...

Bending and stretching ideas about!

That is the moment
the magic begins.

"Weedle Bop Tweedle!"

The Dreamweaver spins ....

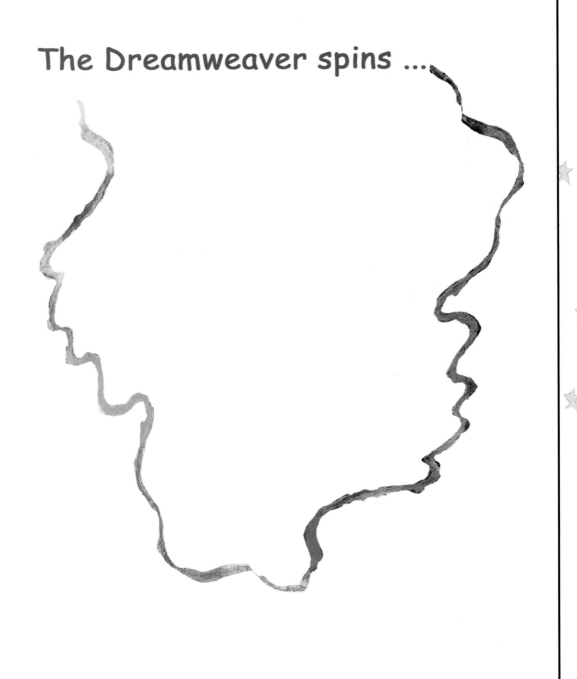

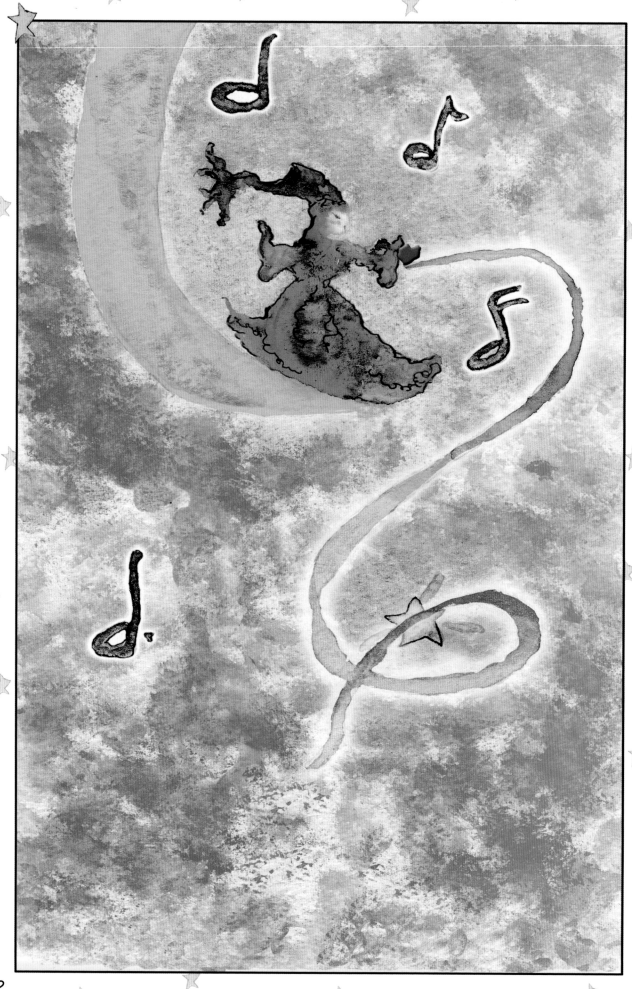

Dancing by moonlight
she captures your dream!

13

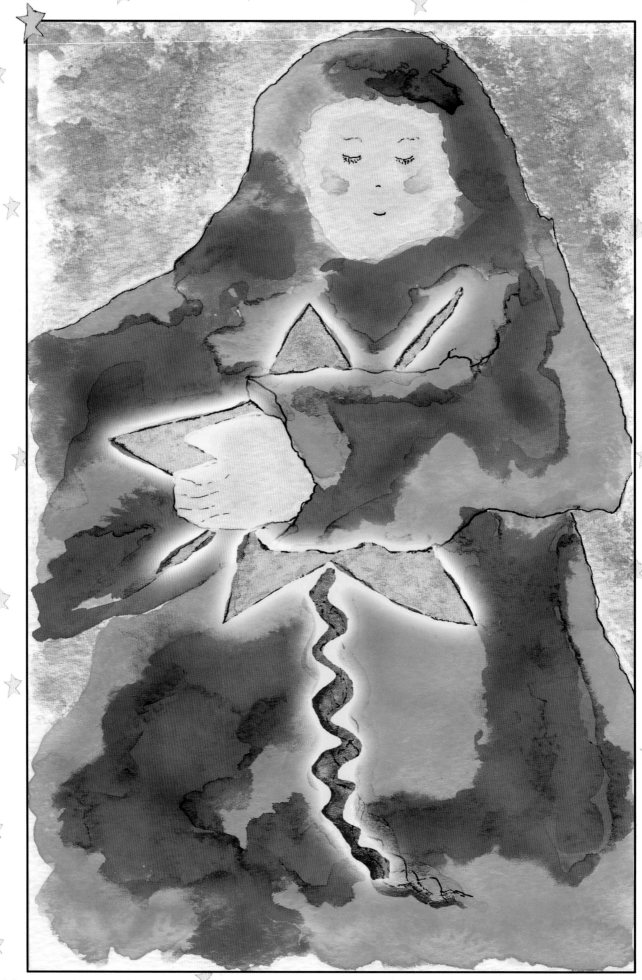

She hugs it ...

and holds it ...

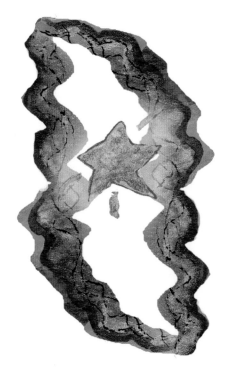

and fashions a seam ...

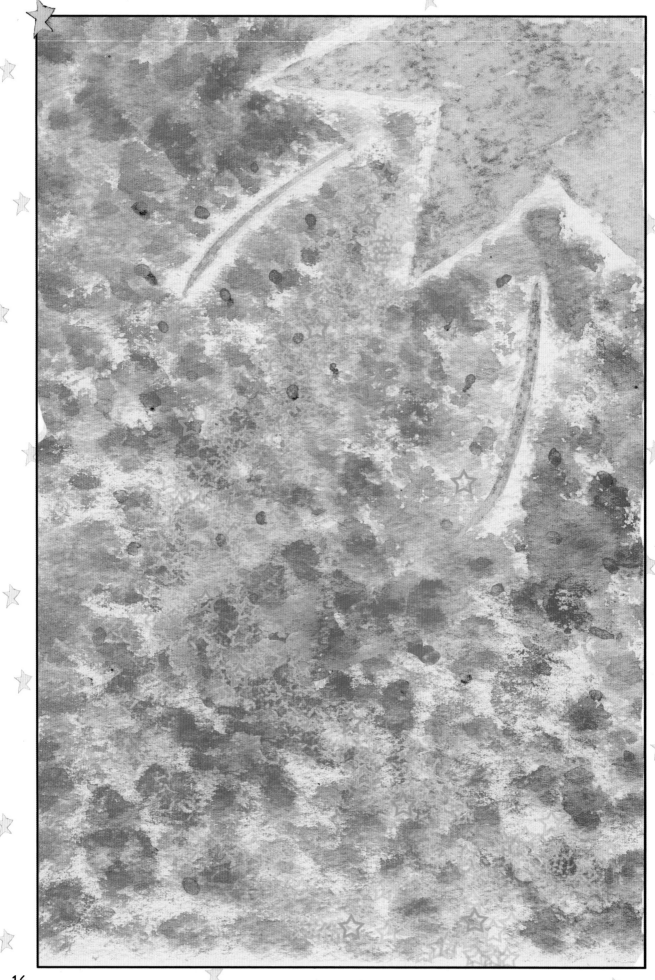

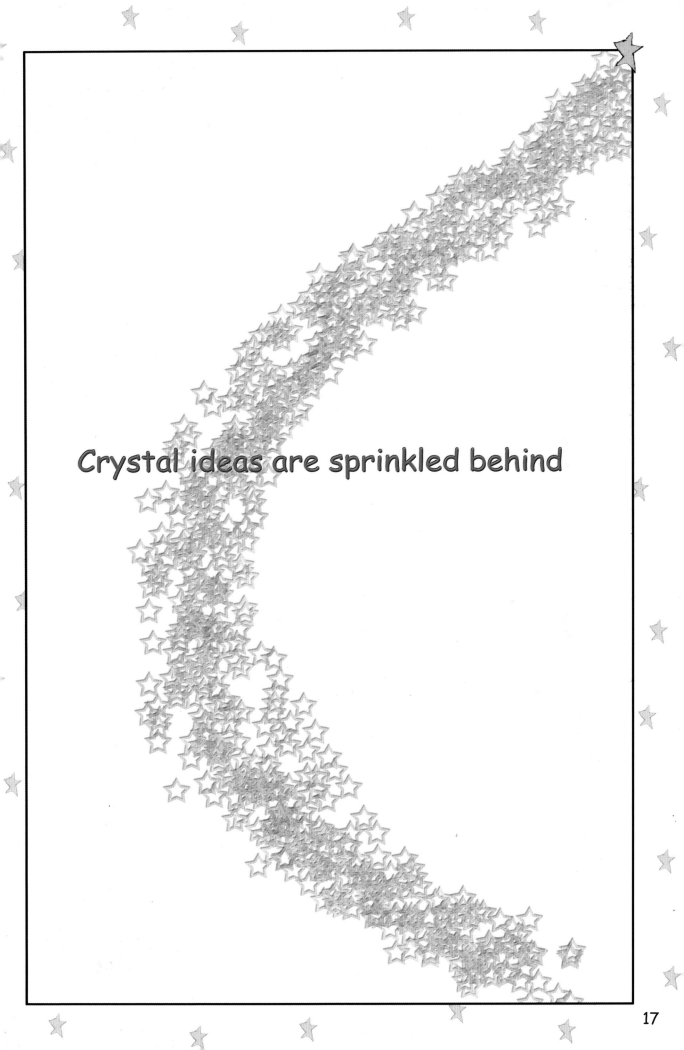

Crystal ideas are sprinkled behind

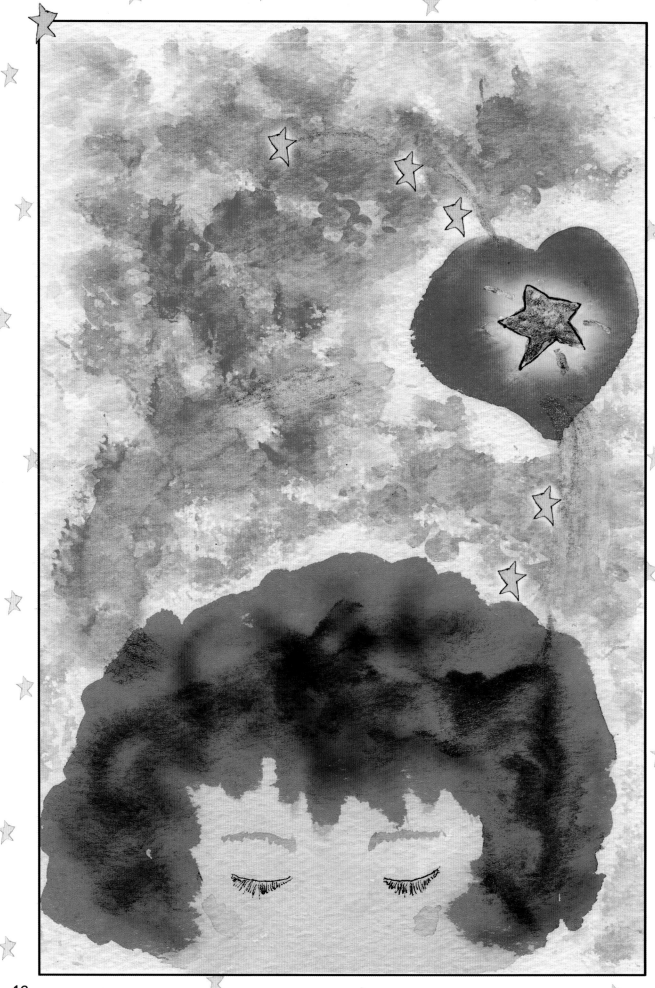

As the dream makes its way

in and out of your mind...

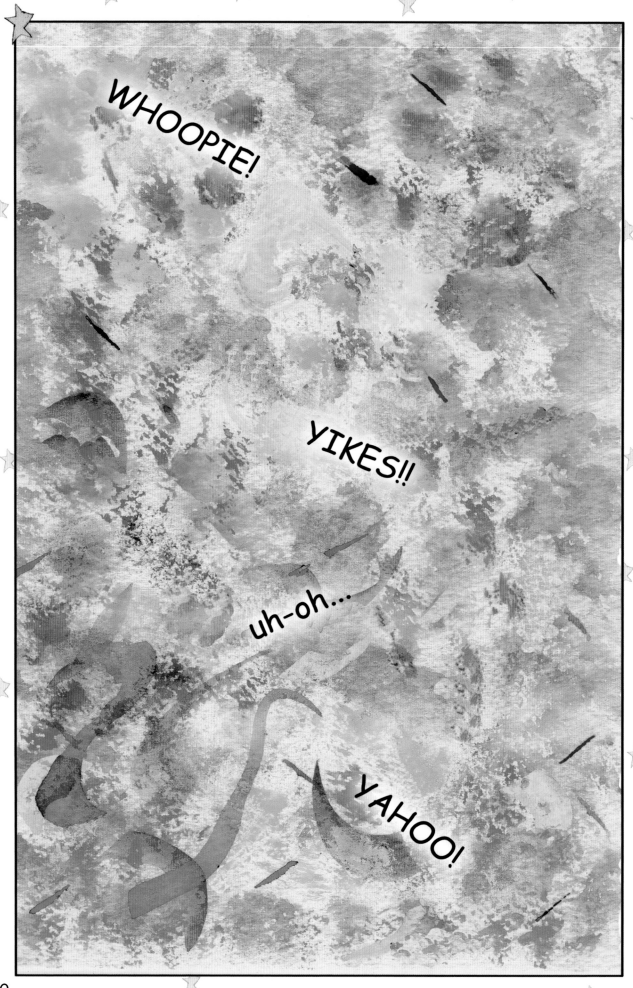

Thoughts tumble-jumble

and circle again,

colored and shaded

from places they've been!

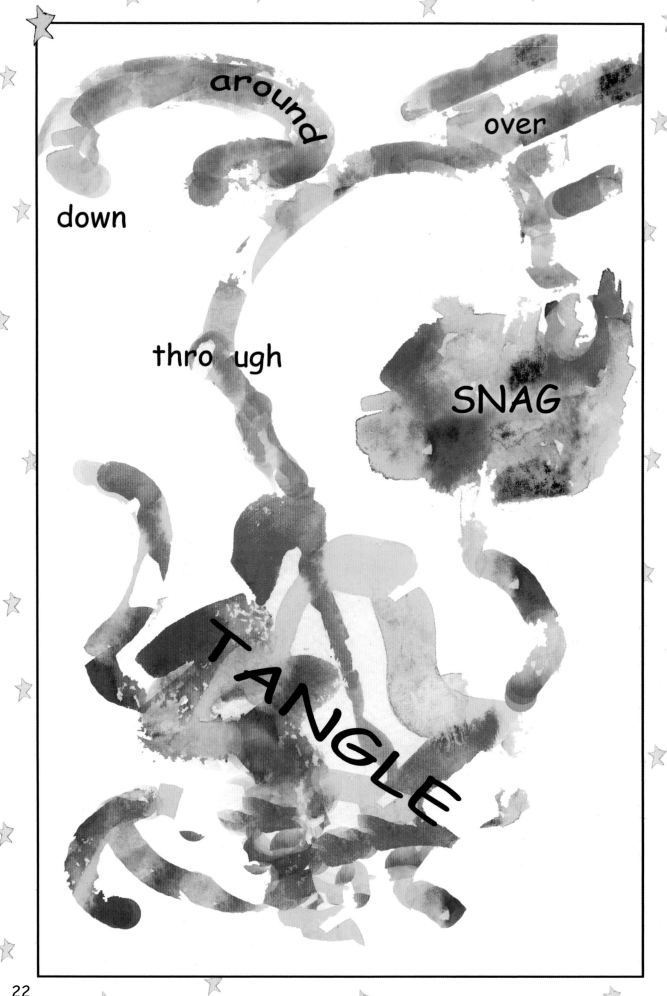

around

over

down

thro ugh

SNAG

TANGLE

Down and around,
lacing over and through,

HERE IS A SNAG,

and a TANGLE or two ...

24

"Invite them right in!"

The Dreamweaver knows,

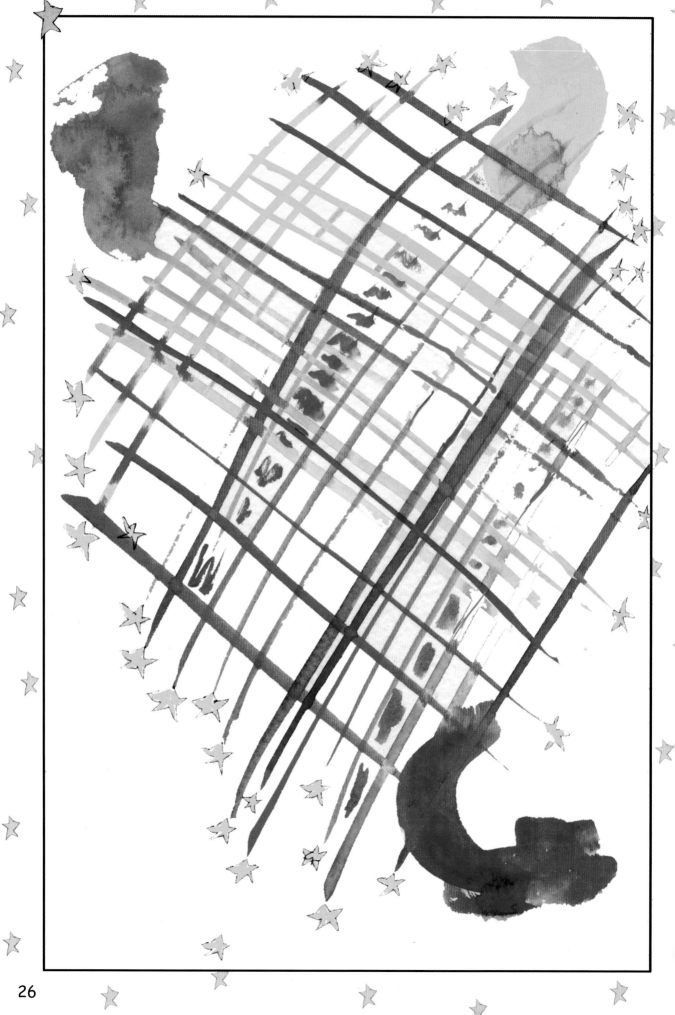

The greatest ideas

just follow their nose!!!

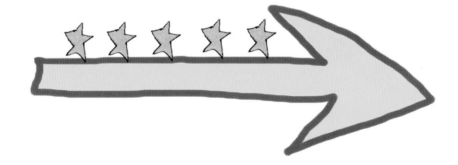

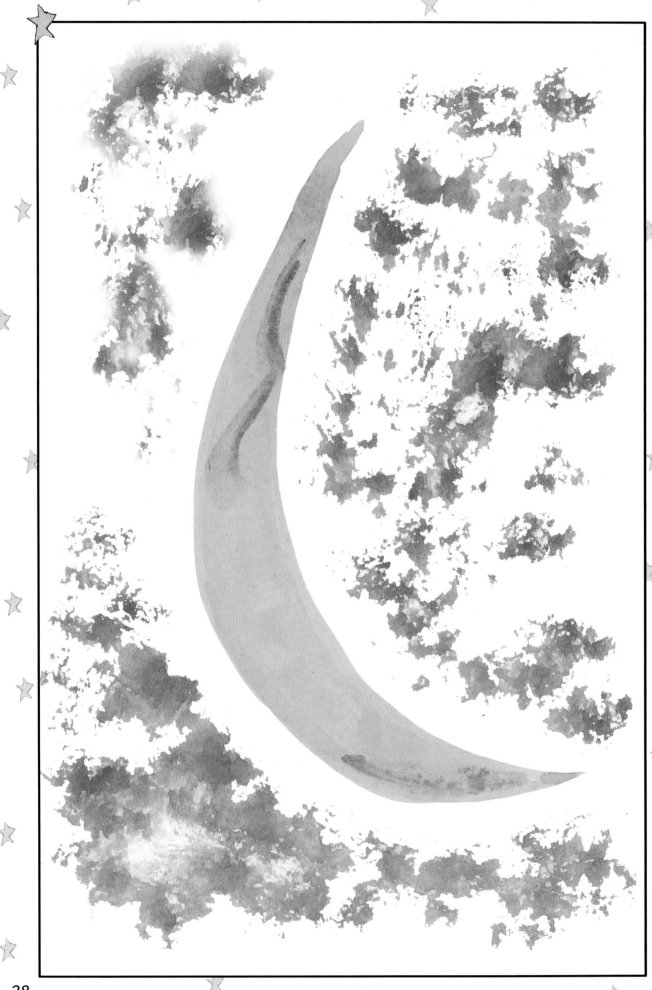

Some take a lifetime,

Others can see

from the very beginning

where they want to be.

There are those who discourage

the dreamers of dreams.

Their words will be little and tidy and clean.

Their fears will seem Sensible,
Simple,
and
Sound.

They'll rework and lasso your dreams to the ground.

"Don't listen!",

the Dreamweaver
merrily sings.

Dreams come to life

when you give them their wings!

When the Dreamweaver sees

it is time to be through,

She whispers a secret

known only to you.

It is in that instant

the clouds disappear.

and there is your

Dream

hanging sparkling and clear!

In case you've not noticed

I'll give you a clue.

The dream here is yours

and the Dreamweaver -

YOU!

What COLOR is your Dream?

. . . Book Ordering Information . . .

It's pretty simple.

Check your leading bookstore or go to

www.kittiebgoods.com

to place an order. While you're there,
walk through my store stocked FULL
of goodies! You will meet some new friends,

If you don't love me because I'm beautiful,
you're the only one . . .

find some unusual and fun things to purchase,
     (who are Freebox Friends?)

explore new ideas, sights and sounds!
(What is Emma's Dilemma? Care to take a walk to
Marmalade Manor? Shoebox Theatre is waiting for YOU!)

. . . and MUCH MUCH more . . .

See you in the funny papers!

Meow